MAKING SENSE OUT OF DOLLARS

THE SIMPLETON'S GUIDE TO UNDERSTANDING THE AMERICAN ECONOMY

by Brian Shellabarger

Published by Lulu
October 2007

Email Contact: books@brianshellabarger.com

Copyright © 2007 by Brian Shellabarger

All rights reserved

1st Edition
First Printing, October 2007

ISBN: 978-1-4357-0193-9

ACKNOWLEDGEMENTS

I wish to express a very sincere thanks to those who voiced their opinion that the contents and text written here should be distributed as a printed book. Many hours went into the creation and research of this text, and were it not for the constant encouragement of friends and acquaintances who felt strongly that the text would prove valuable to others, I probably would never have undertaken this small project.

TABLE OF CONTENTS

INTRODUCTION

—

I'm constantly amazed at how few Americans really understand the economic news that shows up in the headlines nearly every day. In fact, most of the people *reporting* the news don't even understand what it means,

I'm convinced, however, that people really do *want* to understand, but most people don't have the patience or the time to really sit through the complex theoretical textbook approach that's traditionally used to teach economics. The tragedy is that while this may be the preferred approach for *teaching* economics, it's probably the worst approach for *learning* economics. The average American wants merely to gain a basic understanding of what causes the wheels of our economy to work without being forced to memorize complex theories, formulas, or the foreign-language of economists.

If you're that person, then this book is for you.

In writing this book, I assume you do have at least a basic understanding of finance. If you know what interest is, for example, you shouldn't have any trouble following along.

In other words, I've tried to make sure the concepts in this book can be understood and enjoyed by teenagers, college-students, parents, and business executives alike.

My hope is that you will finish this book with a conversational-level understanding of inflation, debt, the dollar, the stock market, supply and demand, and how all of these impact your daily life. I also hope it will make the news more interesting, since you should start to understand the impact of common events (such as interest-rate changes from the Federal Reserve). I also hope it will make you more aware of the impact of having politicians in office who do not understand these things (I fear many don't).

Always remember that economics is more a collection of theories than an exact science. Nobody knows for sure how the economy works. In fact, even the most foundational principles regarding how free-market economics work (such as "the law of supply and demand") are still just theories in their fundamental nature.

I mention this because I want to make it clear that, even though what's presented in this book are fairly accepted universal truths, in the world of economics, there's actually no such thing. What we accept as "truth" has merely yet to be disproven. There are simply too many factors driving a modern economy to *prove* why anything happens, so we go with our past experience and our best guesses to explain things and create theories.

CHAPTER 1: SUPPLY AND DEMAND

There's really only one economic principle worth understanding. All other economic theories and ideas stem from "The law of supply and demand". Once you understand this concept, you'll have a much greater ability to understand the wheels that keep the economy moving. In fact, the concepts discussed in all of the other chapters in this book are derived from this foundational principle.

In essence, the law of supply and demand states that as the demand for an item goes up, the price goes up right along with it. If demand for an item should suddenly fall, the price will go down. So why is it the law of *supply* and demand? Because demand can be determined by "supply". (If there's a shortage of something, people tend to want it more, and thus are willing to pay more).

If I offered you a $20 cheeseburger, you're not likely to buy it. If I offered you a $3 cheeseburger, you'd probably buy it if you were hungry. If I offered you the same cheeseburger for $0.25, you'd probably buy it regardless and save it until you were hungry.

Who decides how much something is worth?

Ask yourself how much a cheeseburger is worth. A dollar? Maybe two? Why is that? Who decides how much a cheeseburger is worth? The answer is the people who buy cheeseburgers do. Sellers can only try and convince you what something is worth, but ultimately, if the seller believes an item is worth more than the purchaser, it won't sell.

Now picture a room full of starving people (all the doors and windows are locked, so nobody can leave). These people need food soon or they're doing to die. Someone figured out a way to enter the room with a cheeseburger in hand. Now, in this circumstance, how much is that same cheeseburger worth?

In other words, the market has only one cheeseburger, but 100 people want it. If this was to happen in real life, and the person in the room was only allowed to sell their cheeseburger to one person, what do you think would happen?

If you said "bidding war", you'd be right. The cheeseburger is worth whatever the richest person in the room is willing to pay. Everyone needs the cheeseburger, but only the wealthiest person will get it. Because there's only one person supplying the item that's needed, the seller can essentially charge whatever they want because they have the only item that's needed by everyone. (Side note: This is known as a "monopoly".)

Now let's say ten people enter the room with 500 cheeseburgers each to sell to the 100 hungry people. Do you think people will be willing to pay as much? There are 5,000 burgers to go around now, there's no need to enter crazy bidding wars, and in fact, since it's clear everyone is going to eat, the sellers may not even be able to sell all of them and will probably start competing with one another on price. Thus the value of the cheeseburgers is much smaller (supply went higher than demand, so the price went down substantially).

Fortunately, we don't have to enter bidding wars every time we go to the grocery store, but we do still see examples of this law while we're there. For example, consider for a moment why the price of a gallon of milk changes on an almost daily basis. (Less milk available on the market means stores have to charge more so they don't run out).

So, to put it simply, supply and demand is really all about finding that sweet spot between "how much can I charge for this item" and "how much are people willing to pay". Supply and demand dictates that the amount people are willing to pay will change constantly based on how many of those items are available and how bad they need it.

Consider the following scenarios to hopefully make this concept clear (it really does need to be understood, so bear with me).

Example 1: No demand means lots of supply, which leads to lower prices.

Joe has just invented a new gasoline additive (let's call it Joe Juice) that makes cars run smoother. Joe decides Joe Juice is so great, he's going to sell it for $100 a quart. Unfortunately, nobody is buying it for that price, even though store shelves are full of the item. Joe quickly realizes that $100 is just too much, and he's going to have to lower the price. He experiments with lots of

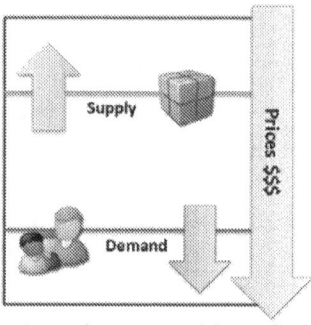

As supply goes up and demand goes down, prices will decrease.

different prices, and eventually realizes that when he charges $10 a bottle, people are willing to buy one bottle a month to put in their car.

Example 2: Higher demand means lower supplies and higher prices.

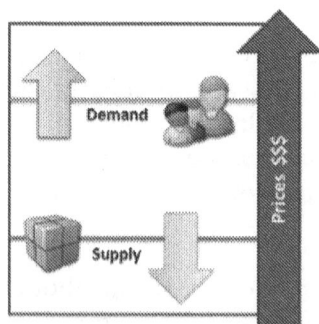

As demand goes up and supplies go down, prices will increase.

Someone discovers that if you use two bottles of Joe Juice, your gas mileage will increase to 100 miles per gallon. Suddenly, people are buying Joe Juice so quickly nobody can get their hands on it anymore. The second a bottle hits the store shelf, it's gone in minutes. Joe realizes his consumers see increased value in his item and raises the price. When he sets the price to $200 a bottle, sales finally slow down enough for Joe to keep up with the demand. He's making lots of money, and consumers are happier because they can generally find Joe Juice on store shelves when they need it (and they're willing to pay for it).

The point from these examples is that a free market will regulate prices based on supply and demand. People will either refuse to buy something that's too expensive; or they'll buy *all* of something that's too cheap (making the item impossible to acquire). When you find the middle ground, store shelves have just enough, consumers will be able to buy the things they need while still feeling like they're getting a good deal (based, of course, on how badly they need item).

It should be stressed that in a "monopoly" situation (one person has all of a particular item that's needed by everyone), all bets on pricing are off. They can and will charge whatever they want because consumers have no choice but to pay. (This is why the government carefully enforces anti-trust laws). Competition, on the other hand, spreads the demand across several different companies and gives consumers choices. Ultimately, competition will always drive the price of an item down.

CHAPTER 2: THE U.S. DOLLAR: THE KING OF CURRENCIES

THE DOLLAR: ONCE BACKED BY GOLD; NOW BACKED BY NOTHING.

Until 1975, the dollar was backed by gold reserves. This means for every dollar the government printed, they had to have a certain amount of gold held in reserve. It also meant you knew at any given time exactly how much your dollar was worth. There was something tangible with real value behind every printed dollar.

From 1792 (when the Mint Act was passed) the dollar was "pegged" to about $19 for an ounce of gold. In 1900, the dollar was re-defined – 1oz of gold was worth $20. In 1933, the gold standard was changed again -- 1oz of gold was now worth $35. The changes allowed the government to "balance the checkbook" (so to speak). If they found they didn't have enough gold to cover the number of dollars in circulation, they were effectively faced with two choices. They could A) attempt to acquire more gold, thus maintaining the value of the dollar or B) they could re-define how much gold a dollar was worth to bring the account back into balance. The latter of the two options was effectively a hidden tax on the American people (we'll talk more about that when we discuss inflation), but it certainly was easier and cheaper for the government. I think you can guess which one they chose any time they found themselves short on gold.

Federal Reserve Notes printed during this time carried the obligation "The United States of America will pay to the bearer on demand [some number of] dollars." (or similar text, depending on the year). Since dollars were defined in gold, this was a way for an American citizen to trade their Federal Reserve Notes (paper) for something with real value (gold).

A 1913 $10 bill. The bottom says "Ten Dollars In Gold Coin – Payable to the Bearer On Demand". This bill could be exchanged for about a half-ounce of gold at any federal bank.

By the beginning of the 1960's, the mandated "gold ratio" of 1oz to $35 was becoming more and more difficult to sustain. Gold demand was rising and U.S. Gold reserves were falling, both as a result of the ever increasing trade deficits which the U.S. continued to run with the rest of the world (we'll talk more about why this happens in the next section on inflation).

By 1968, the U.S. was faced with the choice of either eliminating their trade deficits (again, we'll talk more about trade deficits in the next section) or re-valuing the dollar downward to match the real value of gold – again. In other words, we were experiencing heavy inflation, and the government was having a hard time keeping that checkbook in balance.

> **Keep an Eye on Gold**
>
> *Knowing that gold acts as a sort of "universal currency", we can keep an eye on the value of our dollars by knowing how much gold our dollar will buy. As the price of gold goes up, we know inflation is happening.*

Instead of changing the amount of gold that was pegged to a dollar as had been the custom in these cases, President Nixon decided to ignore the international obligation of the U.S. to redeem its Dollar in Gold. On August 15th, 1971, Nixon closed the "Gold Window". The last link between Gold and the Dollar was gone. By the end of 1974, Gold had soared from $35 to $195 an ounce, and currently trades well above $700 an ounce. Dollars were no longer priced in gold; gold was now priced in dollars. The government could now effectively print as much money as they wanted or needed without having to come up with gold to back the currency.

The promise of redemption also vanished from the face of each Federal Reserve Note. Thus, on their faces Federal Reserve Notes became, in the apt description of banking expert John Exter, an "I.O.U. Nothing" currency. Modern American dollars are backed by nothing and mean nothing.

Dollars continue to have value in the international market because of the trust the world has in the fiscal responsibility of the United States government (who deals exclusively in this un-backed currency). By that, I mean they have confidence in our government's ability continue to pay the interest on our national debt and keep inflation from rising too rapidly – they trust that our government is not printing lots of money. Since the gold-standard was removed, our government has traditionally been pretty good at this – proven by the fact that the dollar has held up well against foreign markets, and many foreign banks choose to hold dollars in reserve because they know the U.S. government will still be around tomorrow. (Note: currencies backed only by confidence in a government are known as "fiat currencies").

To put it simply, the modern dollar is nothing more than an agreement on a system of barter. We all know the paper the dollar printed on isn't worth anything (you can't make anything more valuable than a paper airplane out of it, and you certainly can't eat it), but since we've accepted that it should be used as the foundation for bartering, we perceive it has value.

WHAT IS AN EXCHANGE RATE?

In the simplest terms, the exchange rate is the amount of foreign currency you can purchase with your dollar. Exchange rates are constantly changing as the value of our currency and other world currencies changes on a second-by-second basis. If two currencies were both backed by gold, the price of each currency (when compared to the other) would never change because they had agreed on a standard to anchor their value.

Since the dollar is backed by nothing but the world's confidence in our government, we can instantly gauge that confidence by looking at how much money (in a foreign currency) someone is willing to trade us for our dollar. For example, if Euro's are "expensive" (e.g. it costs us $1.20 to buy one Euro), then we know that confidence in the dollar is low. Conversely, if Euros are cheap (e.g. $1.00 buys 1.5 Euros) then we know confidence in the dollar is high. Remember. If the world starts to suspect the U.S. is printing lots of money, or that it might not be able to pay the interest rate on our national debt, they're probably not going to be willing to pay as much for a dollar, fearing that it might not be as "sure" as they thought. (Remember the law of supply and demand? Demand for U.S. dollars increases with confidence, and thus the price goes up).

CALCULATING THE VALUE OF THE DOLLAR USING THE DOLLAR INDEX

The dollar index was established in 1973 with a starting value of 100. The index measure the value of the US dollar compared to a weighted average of 6 different foreign currencies (the Euro, the Japanese Yen, the British Pound, the Canadian Dollar, the Swedish Krona, and the Swiss Franc).

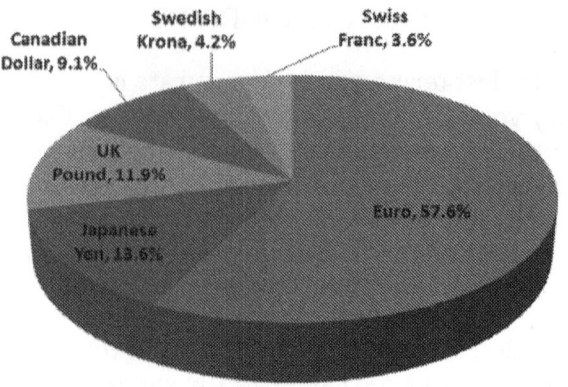

Currencies used to calculate the US Dollar Index and their respective weight

By following the "average" we can know the value of the dollar compared to what it was back in 1973 when it was established and the dollar was considered strong. Thanks to a congress who had balanced the budget and kept spending under control, from 2000 to 2003 the dollar index was very strong, ranging from 100 to 120. World-confidence in the ability of our government to manage spending without the need to print more money was very high. This all changed around 2001/2002 when the republican controlled congress and Whitehouse began spending at an unprecedented rate. In fact, they've outspent the budget so significantly, the world is now starting to lose confidence that the U.S. can continue this "drunken spending spree" (as critics have called it) without printing massive quantities of money. As a result of the loss of confidence, the dollar index is currently trading lower than it ever has historically.

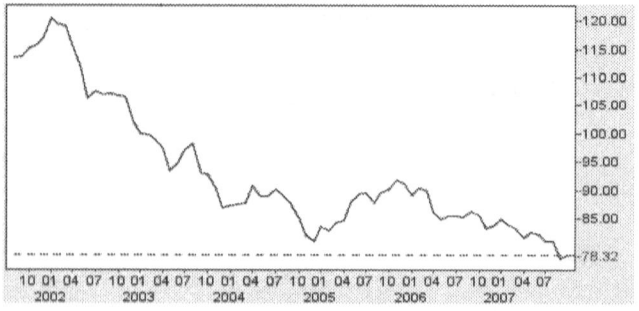

US Dollar Index over the last 5 years

WHY DO WE CARE WHAT THE WORLD THINKS OF THE DOLLAR?

First, because as a country, we spend more than we make – and if we want the world to keep lending us money, they must continue to remain confident that our government can make the interest-payments on-time. Since printing money doesn't give the government spending-power over the long term, real loans from real institutions are required in order for us to maintain a negative balance on our spending. This is no different than if you were to run in the negative each month in your personal finances. You would have to borrow money from someone – let's say Visa. If you started missing your minimum payment each month, Visa would stop lending you more money – so would everyone else.

Second, because we are now part of a fully global economy. We import so much of what we use. Therefore, we must continue to have strong purchasing power on the world market or the things we import (65%+ of our consumable goods) will go up in price. Most Americans can't afford to have the cost of their goods go up very much without it having a real impact on their life, so it's important to keep the dollar strong so that we can continue to import foreign goods at the prices we're used to. Since American's are no longer willing to work for the same wages that other people in the world are willing to work for, we can't simply go back to the system wherein we make everything domestically (If we did, we'd either have to all take a huge pay-cut, or pay more for our goods to cover the increased cost of labor to produce them).

WHY THE WORLD CARES ABOUT THE DOLLAR

Confidence in the US government has been so high over the last 50 years, the world has, for the most part, adopted the dollar as the US world currency standard (until very recently, it has proven to be the most stable currency in the world). In fact, the US government has even managed to make sure valuable world resources are priced in dollars (this means if the dollar falls in value, the US doesn't have to pay a penalty as a result!)

It's also important to understand that the world economy is actually backed by US dollars. Since there's no longer enough gold in the world to back all of the wealth and currency that's floating around, the US dollar has historically been used as a "reserve" currency for foreign countries. It's incredible, and very frightening, to think that our "fake" currency has become so powerful, and so well respected, that countries are willing to hold dollars in lieu of gold as a means of guaranteeing the value of their own currency! In this scenario, imagine the impact on the world economy if the value of the dollar continues downward. Foreign banks will feel increased pressure to sell their dollars and exchange them for something more solid (perhaps the Euro?) – and selling only furthers the downward spiral.

Hopefully you're starting to get an understanding of why the world economy is so fragile.

The point is that the effects of the US Dollar value going up or down are literally felt by the entire world, which is why the rest of the world pays so much attention to the economic and political affairs in the US.

WHAT FACTORS INFLUENCE THE VALUE OF THE DOLLAR?

This is a complicated question. In the end, there's really only one factor (as mentioned above) – confidence in the US government. However, we can break this down to a more granular level.

The main things that impact the value of the dollar are trade balances, politics, future entitlements to citizens (social secure, Medicare, etc.), interest rates, American consumer activities, the housing market, industry productivity and costs, US capital markets, the economy, the weather, inflation data, etc.

CHAPTER 3: INFLATION

—

EXPLANATION OF INFLATION

Now that we know what a dollar actually is, it's much easier to understand inflation. In the simplest terms, inflation is what happens when the value of the dollar goes down in relation to the cost of "goods". Remember all those stories your grandfather told you about all the things a nickel could buy back in his day? I think we all know a nickel isn't worth what it once was. Inflation is what causes money to be worth "less" over time.

HOW INFLATION IS MEASURED

In the simplest of terms, inflation is calculated by looking at how much normal consumer-purchased items cost at a given time. We can do this because some things never really increase in value, they just go up in price (a good indicator that inflation is happening) An example of this would be the price of a postage stamp. The service is still exactly the same as it was 50 years ago, but over the last 50 years, the price of a stamp has risen from 4 cents (in 1958) to 41 cents (today). This, combined with looking at equivalent prices for thousands of others items, is a good indication that a dollar is worth less today than it was back in 1958. On the surface, this seems silly. Of *course* the dollar is worth less than it was 50 years ago. But what we're really interested in is whether or not this is happening on a month-by-month basis, and if so, exactly how much?

One of the tricks in measuring inflation is to make sure we're only measuring the right kind of items. If you measure something that really does fluctuate in price (oil, for example) then you might be fooled into thinking inflation is happening when, in reality, it may simply be that the demand for a particular item is going up (and that's what's driving the price up).

This is where the "Consumer Price Index" (CPI) comes in. Every month the Bureau of Labor Statistics (BLS) surveys the cost of thousands of consumer goods across more than 200 categories (food, housing, apparel, transportation, medical care, recreation, education, good & services, etc.) and uses the data to generate the Consumer Price Index (CPI). You've probably heard of this index. Examples of items included in the survey include the cost of a pizza, the price of a cell phone service plan, the price of an average SUV, the cost of a box of tissues, the price of an airline ticket, the price of a hamburger, etc.

In order to understand the actual numbers produced by the CPI, let's assume (for fun) that the index consists of one item -- and that item was $1.00 in 1984.... This would mean the index (if this was the only item in the index) would have been 100 in 1984. If that same item today was $1.80, the index would rise to 180. This gives us a very simple way of knowing how inflation is doing, relatively speaking, on a month-to-month basis.

Because it's so diverse, the CPI is considered to be extremely accurate by financial professionals. If a new good or service is introduced, it usually takes several years before it's even considered for inclusion in the CPI.

The "core" CPI excludes food and energy prices, since those are constantly fluctuating. This core CPI is the index most investors pay attention to. Because the CPI is tracked across so many different categories, we can get a snapshot at any given time as to whether or not there's inflation pressure from one of these areas that might not have affected the others, yet. (For example, we might see the price of corn going up, but the price of beef staying the same. Using this information, we can assume there will be "inflation pressure" on beef because cows eat corn and, therefore, it will eventually cost more to produce beef.)

When the CPI is published, it's generally as a number reflecting the increase in inflation over the previous 12-month period. (So the numbers for August are for Aug-06 to Aug-07).

A steadily rising CPI is a sure indicator that inflation is happening. In general, the CPI is expected to rise 1% to 3% annually. Any less than this and it's a sign that deflation may be happening. Any more than this and it's a sign that inflation is moving quicker than normal. Every month before new CPI indicators are published, the market collectively holds their breath. These numbers have a *big* impact on investor confidence.

Hopefully, it's understood that calculating inflation and the CPI is actually much more complicated than outlined here, plus there are several other indicators that can be used to measure inflation, but for the purpose of this book, this explanation should be enough to understand the general idea.

HOW DOES INFLATION AFFECT ME?

Hopefully, the answer is obvious: inflation means your dollar has less purchasing power.

That postage stamp that used to cost 4 cents now costs 41 cents. That candy-bar that used to cost a nickel now costs 60 cents. That movie that used to cost 50 cents now costs 8 dollars. This means you, Average-Joe-American, need to make more money in order to compensate for the increased cost of goods.

Grandpa will tell you about how great a nickel was back in his day, but he usually forgets to mention that he only brought home $100 a week. It's all relative – and as long as wages increase along-side the cost of goods, everyone comes out okay.

PROTECTING YOUR HARD-EARNED MONEY AGAINST INFLATION

There are several strategies that will typically help preserve your "wealth" against the plundering of inflation. First, let's look at a common mistake nearly everyone makes.

Most Americans insist on keeping their money in low-return savings accounts over the long-term. In the context of inflation, this is a huge problem. A typical savings account will usually generate 0.5% to 2% interest on an annual basis. The problem is that inflation is generally no less than 3% every year. This means the bank is adding 2% to your account each year, but the government is taking 3% out. At the end of the year, this leaves us with a bank account that might have a little more cash in it than when we started, but the money will buy "1% less stuff" than when we started. This is why keeping large sums of money in savings accounts long-term is a bad idea – it looks like you're doing well, but you're actually losing money to the "hidden tax" that is inflation (more on this when we talk about what causes inflation).

With this in mind, the only way to beat inflation is to find an investment that generates a higher return than inflation. If inflation averages about 3% per year (closer to 5% over the last few years), we've got to find an investment that will return at least that amount, or more if we want to come out ahead.

Most people, when attempting to battle inflation, like to buy things with "intrinsic value". This means they want to purchase something that's worth "roughly the same" no matter what happens to the dollar. Gold, silver, oil, real-estate, and other such items will always be worth about the same, even if the price changes. An example of this would be the price of a nice suit. In 1850, 1oz of gold would buy you a very nice business suit – valued in that day around $25. In 1955, 1oz of gold would still buy you a very nice business suit, but it was now valued at about $150. In 2007, 1oz of gold will still buy you a very nice suit – today valued at about $700. See the pattern? The gold itself had "intrinsic value" – it's has the same purchasing power

---

today that it had 100 years ago. We certainly can't say that about the dollar.

Since I mentioned real-estate, it might be worth taking a closer look at why real-estate is considered a good "hedge" against inflation. If you picked up a 30-year mortgage back in 1985, you should have roughly 8 years left until your house is paid off. Of course, remember, back in 1985 your dollar was worth roughly twice what it is today (and you probably made about half as much money as you do today). This means your $75,000 house that you picked up in 1985 is worth $150,000 in today's dollars (probably more, because the value of real estate has been going up faster than the dollar declines). Great news, though: It's 2007 and you still have a $75,000 mortgage with a $400 payment – but you live in a house worth a lot more. This is why real-estate is generally considered to be a good way to protect against inflation – you get to use someone else's money over the long term, but you get to keep the thing you bought with the "old-value" money. So while the value of the dollar goes down, the value of your very-expensive asset (your house) stays the same. Just like gold!

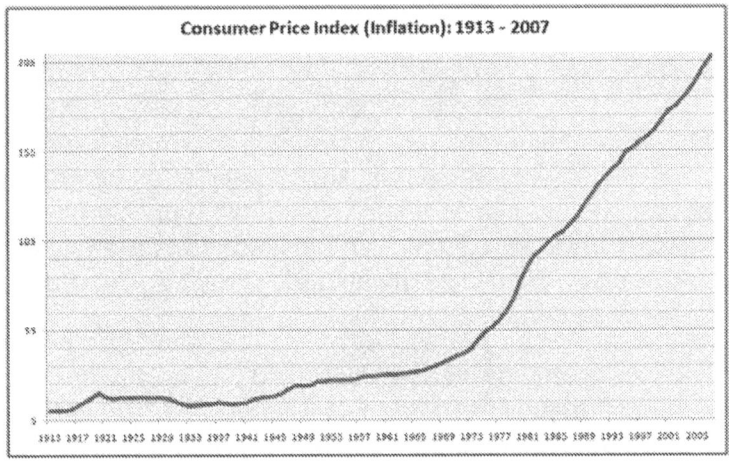

The dollar in 2007 is worth 17% less than it was in 2000 and 85% less than it was in 1960. This means if you don't make 15% more than you made in 2000, you've taken a pay-cut without knowing it. (Source: inflationdata.com)

WHAT CAUSES INFLATION?

Now that we know what inflation actually is, we should probably spend a few minutes at least trying to understand what causes it. Make sure you're sitting down before I give you the answer to this one, because you're not going to believe it........ Are you ready? The answer is: We don't really know.

That's not to say there aren't hundreds (even thousands) of theories out there from leading economists, mathematicians, and brilliant scholars. Everyone's got their own theories for what ultimately causes the value of the dollar to go down (they might all be right) – but nobody can agree on a strategy for preventing it. Different presidents have tried different things with varying degrees of success (even then, economists still argue about the reasons for the success). For this reason, I'm really not going to go into crazy details about what may or may not cause inflation. If you're interested in these theories, there are hundreds of books you can buy that will give you all the gory details.

There are a few things, however, that we know for sure will cause inflation. We'll talk about two of the big ones: printing money and trade deficits.

PRINTING MONEY

Put simply, printing more money will inevitably cause your currency to have less purchasing power. Most people know this, but I'm always a little surprised at how many people don't actually understand why – so I'm going to take a few minutes and explain. We'll use jelly beans and peanuts as an example in order to understand how this happens.

Let's assume I've given my family 10,000 jelly beans to divide amongst themselves. Let's also assume you've given your family 10,000 peanuts to divide up. We've agreed that we will trade each other, as needed, for our treats, and we've agreed that one jelly bean should equal one peanut. This is going along pretty well for a while, with everyone happily exchanging peanuts for jelly beans and jelly beans for peanuts because we've all agreed on their intrinsic value. One day, however, I decide I'm sick of only getting one peanut for every one of my jelly beans. I want more; so I decide to make my own jelly beans (they're easy to make, I've got the recipe) – of course I don't tell my family I'm doing this – and I certainly don't tell you (how mad would you be??). But you begin to suspect something is up when I begin buying more and more peanuts with the jelly beans I made. I've made myself rich (temporarily) because I fooled you into thinking my "currency" was worth more than it really is. Of course, once you realized what was going on, you came back and told my family that, from now on, you want two of my jelly beans for every one of your peanuts. I'm back to square-one. Except now my family is mad at me because they thought their jelly beans were worth one peanut each – now they find out they're only worth half what they used to be worth. I've devalued jelly beans for my entire family because I was greedy. It worked for a little while, but eventually everyone was hurt – except me. I still have those extra peanuts I picked up in the beginning before everyone caught on! In other words, by creating more jelly beans, I indirectly imposed a tax on my other family members. I ended up with more peanuts immediately by forcing them to have less in the long run.

It's no wonder the power to print money is so carefully guarded. Increasing the money supply is effectively a hidden tax on the people. When a currency is backed by assets with intrinsic value (gold) it's impossible for a government to do this (they'd need to acquire more gold before printing more money). However, as we learned in chapter 2, the US Dollar is no longer backed by anything. Therefore, printing more money is a decision the government can make on its own. As if this wasn't confusing enough, in 2006 the government stopped reporting "M3 money supply" (the report used to tell us how much money the government was printing), so we're no longer able to keep tabs on when and how much money the government prints.

TRADE DEFICITS

Another major contributor to inflation is what's known as a "trade-deficit". This means we are importing more goods than we export. If a country imports (buys) more than it exports (sells), the difference has to be made up somehow. In our case, we, as a country, borrow the money to make up the loss. Borrowing money we don't have puts a lot of pressure on the dollar (as we'll learn later when we talk about the national debt).

Lately, the trade deficit has been getting worse (in fact, it's at record highs right now) because, to put it simply, foreign workers are willing to work for less money than American workers. We have a certain lifestyle we're used to. We have a minimum wage. We expect healthcare benefits, vacation-pay, sick-leave, and bagels on Fridays. It simply costs more to pay an American to build a "widget" than it costs to pay someone in China. So, you've got two choices – you can either start demanding that American companies manufacture their products here in the United States, thus increasing the cost of producing the item, thus causing you to have to pay more for your everyday things (but bringing the trade-deficit more in-line so we don't experience as much inflation). Or, you can continue to let other countries create the goods you use every day, thus causing the trade-deficit to widen (and inflation to worsen), but you continue to buy your goods nice and cheap, the way you've always done. A third option would be that we all take a pay-decrease so that we can compete with the overseas work-force (I don't think we need to go into that one – we know what the answer would be). The American people have spoken with their loyalties to cheap goods (as proven by the success of Wal-Mart and others). Thus, the trade deficit gets wider and inflation continues to get worse.

HYPER-INFLATION, STAG-FLATION, AND OTHER SCARY TERMS

You may have heard these (or other) terms at various times, so I wanted to take a second and help you understand what they mean and how you might know if they're happening.

Deflation is the first term that's worth talking about – this effectively means the opposite of inflation (the purchasing power of the dollar goes up, rather than down). This is also considered a negative thing. Consider that inflation is a hidden tax on currency holders and borrowers. Deflation, therefore, would be a hidden tax on lenders and investors. Remember the real-estate example from above – now imagine that same scenario in reverse.

Hyperinflation refers to "out of control" inflation. This happens when a currency loses a significant portion of its value in a short period of time. Prices of goods go up very quickly. The causes are often associated with a rapidly declining trust in a currency (a civil war in a small country, for example, would cause investors to question whether the currency currently being printed in that country would be worth anything if the war goes badly, or an unfavorable leader takes the helm). There's no text-book definition for hyperinflation, but one often-accepted parameter is an inflation rate of 20% to 30% in a single month (which might normally take 5 to 10 years). Hyperinflation is a huge problem because of what we talked about above – inflation is only okay if you can keep wages in-check with the increasing prices of goods. If hyperinflation is occurring, this is impossible, and resources, such as gasoline or food, become very scarce, or very expensive (usually both).

Stagflation is the deadly combination of hyperinflation and a sudden increase in unemployment. In other words, not only does everything suddenly skyrocket in price, but people don't have jobs to earn money to buy goods, anyway. The unemployment is usually a result of an economic slowdown (nothing is being produced because nobody wants to buy the goods).

CHAPTER 4: THE FEDERAL RESERVE

—

WHO OR WHAT IS THE FEDERAL RESERVE?

The Federal Reserve (informally, "The Fed") is the central banking system of the United States. The Federal Reserve is a quasi-private/quasi-government banking system composed of the following:

1. The Board of Governors in Washington D.C. (each of the 7 members are appointed by the President), including the chairman of the Board of Governors (currently, Ben Bernanke, who was appointed by President Bush).
2. The Federal Open-Market Committee (FOMC) – consists of the 7 members of the Board of Governors and 5 representatives from select Federal Reserve Banks who rotate.
3. 12 regional Federal Reserve Banks located in major cities throughout the U.S. – These banks act as fiscal agents for the U.S. Treasury. Each bank has a 9-member board of directors.
4. Several private U.S. banking institutions. Each bank must own a certain amount of stock in their regional federal bank and each has a limited controlling interest in their regional bank.
5. Various advisory councils (such as the Federal Advisory Council).

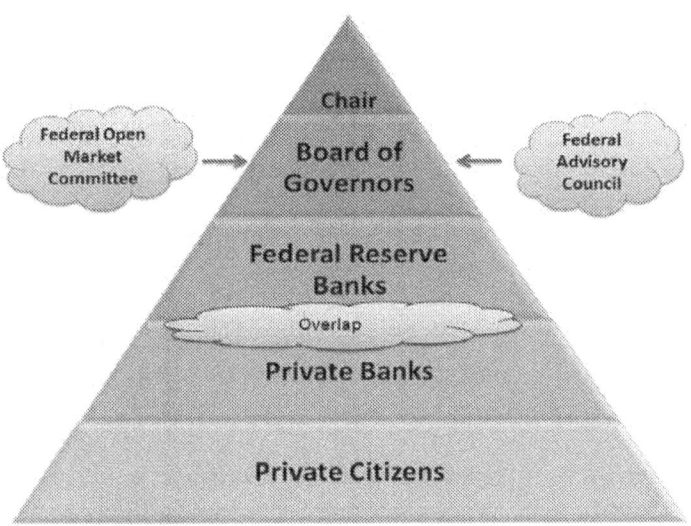

The primary responsibilities of the Federal Reserve are to control and manage the nation's supply of money and manage the federal funds rate and the federal discount rate. (We're going to talk more about all of these). Certainly there are many other smaller roles, but they're the ones most often seen in the headlines, and they're certainly the ones with the biggest direct impact on us, the American consumers.

HOW THE FEDERAL RESERVE CAME TO BE: A BRIEF HISTORY LESSON

Once again, I hope you'll pardon the history lesson, but I think you'll find that the way the Federal Reserve came to be is important in understanding their role.

The Federal Reserve System is actually not the first, or even the second central-bank established in the U.S. The First Bank of the United States (1791-1811) and the Second Bank of the United States (1816-1836) each had twenty year charters. Both were responsible for making loans and issuing currency. There were a large number of people who were not happy with the idea of a "central bank" in either time period – many felt the central banks were corrupt and designed only to benefit the business class at the expense of the average American.

Throughout the late 1800's, several major bank panics occurred wherein big banks were retracting loans, or refusing to renew existing contracts. This provided the perfect political scenario for the creation of a new central banking system despite the negative opinions most citizens expressed over the idea (they felt that granting central authority over money to a single entity was dangerous, and may end up serving only the interests of the ultra-wealthy). However, congress still felt the creation of a permanent central bank was the best way to fix the banking problems. It still wasn't a slam dunk. A group of democrats revolted, demanding the "Money Trust" be destroyed. They were very unhappy about the idea of having private banks operate under the protection of the federal government, and even more unhappy that private institutions would have the power to print money backed by federal obligations. It took the full political influence of Woodrow Wilson and a democratic-majority congress to get the Federal Reserve Act passed in 1913. The new Federal Reserve System became operational a year later.

I wanted to mention all of this because an increasing number of people remain suspicious that the actions of the Federal Reserve are designed to serve the interests of the private financial institutions (many of whom who have controlling interests in the Federal Banks) rather than American consumers at-large.

THE FEDERAL FUNDS RATE AND THE FEDERAL DISCOUNT RATE

When you hear on the news that "The Fed lowered rates" or "The Fed raised rates", they're generally referring to one of two things – either the "Federal Funds Rate" or the "Federal Discount Rate".

The "Federal Funds Rate" is the rate that banks charge each other for overnight loans of "Federal Funds". Federal Funds represent the money that every bank is required to have "on reserve" in order to meet their legal requirements of making sure they have a certain amount of cash on-hand at all times. Banks are constantly loaning this money to each other so that they can stay in compliance (if Bank A has extra money in their "Federal Funds" account, they will loan it to Bank B, who might need a little extra for a day or two in order to cover their legal obligations). The problem for the Fed is that they can't mandate how much one bank charges another for a loan (it's a free market), therefore, this rate is actually completely determined by the market itself. However, the Fed controls the rate artificially through "Open Market Operations" (which we're going to learn about in just a second, so hang on to that term).

The Federal Funds rate matters to you because an increase in the Federal Funds Rate discourages banks from borrowing money, causing them to build up more reserves, and thus makes them less willing to lend you money (in other words, it makes interest rates higher when you walk in to get a loan from your bank). Reducing the Federal Funds Rate has the opposite effect and encourages banks to lend more money by giving you better rates. Remember the law of supply and demand we talked about in Chapter 1? It drives all of this.

The Federal Reserve also sets the "Federal Discount Rate". This is also sometimes known as the "key interest rate". This is the rate that banks pay to borrow money directly from The Fed and generally becomes the 'going rate' for loans between banks. Once again, even though The Fed can't mandate interest rates, they can raise or lower the bar based on their price. If The Fed makes their money cheaper, the banks are expected to match that rate (or they won't get any business from other banks). Conversely, if The Fed wants to raise rates, they simply charge more (thus allowing competing banks to charge a little more as well). In other words, the rate the Fed charges for money is always the "rate to beat" on the street. However, and this is important, banks almost never borrow money directly from the Fed (even if they have to pay a slightly higher interest rate from another bank to avoid it) because borrowing money from The Fed sends a negative signal to the market that they may be desperate for cash and can't get the money any other way.

Once again, this is important because as money costs more for banks to acquire, they will pass those costs on to you, the person on the end who actually uses the money. Higher rates for banks mean higher rates for you.

Both of these rates influence the "Prime" interest rate, which is usually about 3 percent higher than the Federal Funds Rate. Prime is the rate most banks charge when you apply for a loan (assuming you have good credit). Therefore, as The Feds change rates, the "cost of money" changes accordingly.

The Federal Reserve usually adjusts these rates by 0.25% or 0.50% at a time in order to encourage or discourage spending and economic activity. See below on why the Fed cares about interest rates to understand more about why they would want to do this.

CAREFULLY REGULATING THE NATION'S MONEY SUPPLY

One of the key roles of the Federal Reserve is control of the nation's money supply in order to ensure that money is flowing through the economy at the correct price. This is done by engaging in trading activities with major financial institutions (such as Goldman Sachs, Morgan Stanley, Bear Stearns, etc.). Examples of these types of activities include lending money, borrowing money, buying securities, or selling securities.

The Federal Reserve has two main tools for regulating the supply of money in the U.S. Both are known as "Open Market Operations". It's important to understand that the "supply of money" is not the same thing as the "amount of money". Supply refers to the amount of money *available for borrowing* at a given time. When economic times get difficult, money can become scarce, and it's the job of the Federal Reserve to make sure money continues to flow freely, and at the "target" price of the Federal Discount Rate. If not enough money is available, interest rates go too high. If too much money is available, interest rates go too low. By adjusting the amount of money available to the banks, The Fed can effectively dictate the market-price of money.

The first thing The Fed can do to ensure interest rates remain at the target level is by entering into "repurchase agreements" (repos). A "repo" is essentially a short-term loan from The Fed to one of the major financial institutions. The institution is required to put up collateral to collect the money, and when the loan expires, the collateral is returned and the institution pays back the original loan with fees and interest. The length of the loan can be anywhere from 1 to 65 days, but it's usually less than a week. Providing these short-term loans to banks temporarily increases the money supply in the banking system (and lowers interest rates). Of course, the effect is only temporary because the terms on the loans are usually very short. Should The Fed decide the money supply is flowing too easily (and interest rates are getting too low), they can also engage in "reverse repos" wherein the banks will loan money to the federal government for a short period of time. This has the effect of temporarily reducing the supply of money and raising interest rates. Once again, if this sounds like the law of supply and demand, you're exactly right.

Injecting money is not the same as printing money.

When you hear about The Fed "injecting money" into the banking system, this is typically what they're doing. It's very, very important to realize that they are not "printing money" in these instances. They are simply making sure banks have continued access to cash, which is needed to keep the wheels of the economy moving. The money is returned to The Fed within a few days and these actions typically have no impact on inflation.

Through careful and constant lending and borrowing (artificially controlling the supply and demand for money) The Fed can control the market-rate.

How The Feed Keeps Interest Rates at the Target

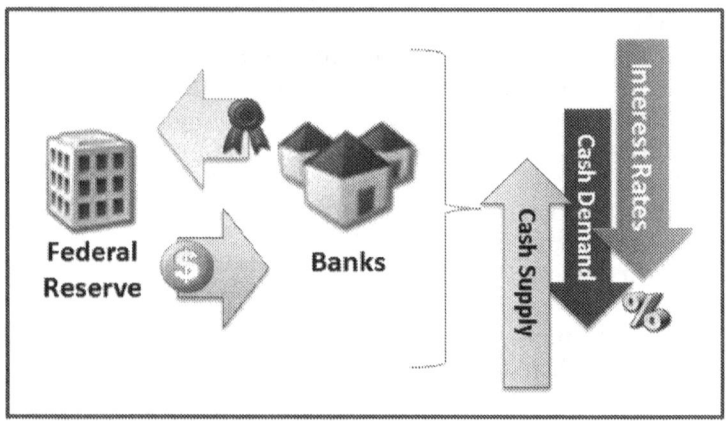

Nudging the market interest rate up.

The Federal Reserve lends cash to banks in exchange for securities (held as collateral) for a few days. The effect is an increase of available cash in the overall market, which causes demand for cash to decrease and money becomes cheaper (the end result is that interest rates go down).

Second, they can perform an "outright transaction". This is when The Fed buys securities (such as bonds) from one of these financial institutions. They do so by depositing newly created money into the bank accounts. In this instance, the resulting increase to the nation's money supply is permanent (in other words, they have effectively printed electronic money). They also have the ability to sell treasuries outright, resulting in the reverse effect (shrinking the nation's money supply) – although this is almost unheard of in modern times.

WHY YOU (AND THE FED) CARE ABOUT INTEREST RATES

There are serious advantages and disadvantages to raising and lowering interest rates, which is why the job of keeping the correct balance is constantly debated.

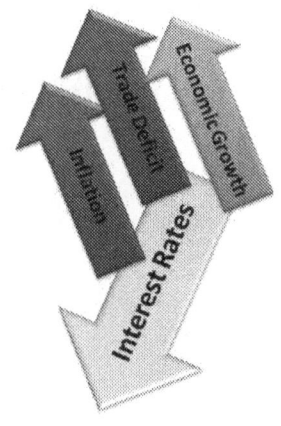

Lower interest rates (or "cheap money") stimulate the economy by making it easier for consumers and businesses to buy and expand – at the same time, lower interest rates contribute heavily to inflation, because cash is freely available and consumers and businesses can actually "out-spend" economic production. This means too much money is floating through the system – and if the U.S. isn't in a position to produce enough goods for consumers to spend their money on, consumers will buy more imported good, thus causing the trade-deficit to increase (we talked about why that contributes to inflation in the last chapter).

On the other hand, higher interest rates slow the economy by making money more expensive, and effectively discouraging purchases and expansion. This has the reverse effect on inflation, and actually slows it down. Less money is available to buy imported goods and the trade deficit actually improves.

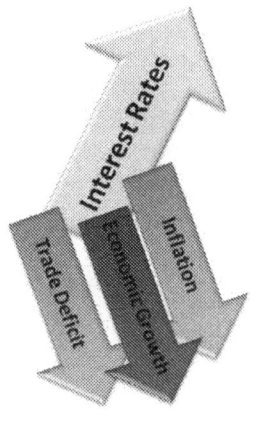

With such tight control over the cost of money, The Fed can carefully dictate the pace of economic growth (and resulting inflation). As a general rule, when The Fed suspects inflation is growing faster than normal (due to a booming economy), interest rates are raised to slow spending and bring inflation back to a more controlled rate. On the other hand, if The Fed suspects inflation may have some room for an increase without damaging the economy, they will lower interest rates to encourage economic growth, create new jobs, etc. It's a delicate dance.

CHAPTER 5: THE NATIONAL DEBT

—

OVERVIEW OF THE NATIONAL DEBT

The national debt really took a firm hold in the lives of Americans after World War II, when we found ourselves having to finance large portions of the war. Ever since then, the United States has spent significantly more money than we earn. It's actually pretty easy to understand this concept when you think of it in terms of a household balance sheet. If the total of your monthly bills ends up being more than your paycheck, this is known as a "budget deficit". To deal with a budget deficit, you basically have two choices.

Option 1) Cut spending – move to a smaller house, get rid of cable TV, or stop eating out so much. In effect, you would do whatever was needed in order to avoid borrowing money to get you through the month.

Option 2) Pay what you can and put the rest on the Visa. Obviously, this will make next month a little more difficult since your minimum payment to Visa will go up, but for now, the bills are paid and you don't have to worry about money for a little while longer. In fact, as long as you can continue to make your minimum monthly payment to Visa on time, they're likely to continue to increase your limit as high as you want. This means we can continue down this path for quite a while! Until, of course, the amount we are paying in interest (our minimum payment) exceeds the size of our paycheck. We call that "bankruptcy".

Obviously, our government hasn't been choosing option #1 or we wouldn't need to write this chapter.

Once we start down the path of borrowing money to pay our bills, we have "debt". If we choose to later fix our spending habits to bring our "budget deficit" back to a point where we're not borrowing more money every month, the debt we acquired during our spending-spree still remains, and we're still expected to make the minimum monthly payment (of course, if we were approaching our problem responsibly, we would start paying more than the minimum so we could eventually get out from under that debt).

Since our government runs a $300-billion-dollar budget deficit every year, congress has decided that, rather than fix the budget so we spend less, they're going to put the remaining balance on "the Visa", otherwise known as The National Debt.

HOW BIG IS THE NATIONAL DEBT?

The number grows daily. On average, $1.36 billion dollars are added to the national debt every day (that's nearly $1 million every minute). Today, the total debt is nearly $9,000,000,000,000.00. That's nine *trillion* dollars. To put this in perspective, this means every man, woman, and child living in the United States would need to come up with

Payoff Term	Your Monthly Payment
Never	$262.91
15 years	$492.15
30 years	$333.75
50 years	$285.25
100 years	$264.53

If we were to begin paying off the debt today

* Assumes the debt will not grow larger.
** Personal share figures calculated by dividing totals by the number of *employed* Americans.

nearly $30,000.00 each in order to get us out of debt. Or, to put it another way, the average family of four would need to come up $120,000 each.

It's important to remember that there's no such thing as government money. It's taxpayer money, and this is a taxpayer debt – your debt. Were it not for the interest on the debt, your taxes would be a lot lower.

WHY IS THIS A PROBLEM?

Just like the person who's deeply in debt on his Visa payment, the United States pays more than $400 billion dollars a year in interest on the national debt. When you compare this to the annual budget of NASA ($16 billion), Education ($61 billion), or transportation ($56 billion), hopefully it starts to make sense why this is a big deal – and as the debt continues to grow at record numbers, so will the amount of money we have to spend on interest.

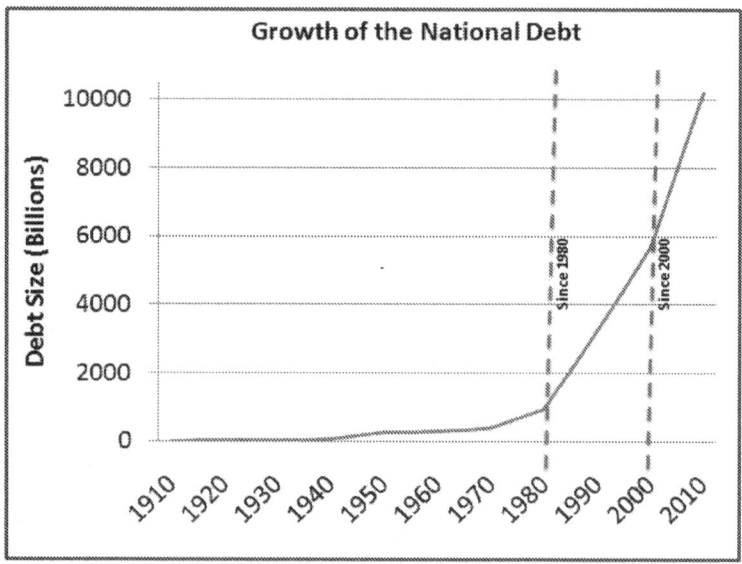

When you further consider the future obligations of the government towards Medicare, Social Security, and other programs, it is estimated that within the next 15 years, the interest we pay on the national debt will exceed the amount of money collected from taxpayers.

Read that again until it sinks it. In just 15 years, the minimum monthly payment on the Visa will be bigger than our paycheck. Once this happens, the lenders will stop raising our credit limit, and the faith in the ability of the government to make good on our debts will plummet (see the first chapter on the dollar to understand what this means). In order to avoid this, the government will have no choice but to print more money, which, as we learned in the chapter on inflation, is really just a hidden way of raising taxes. In this case, printing enough money to solve this problem will likely cause the value of your hard-earned cash to decrease by at least 50%. Could you live on half of what you make today? The government won't have much choice but to force you to do so if the spending continues at projected levels.

Another thing to consider is how rapidly we've increased our spending over the last 10 to 20 years. Consider the chart on the right which shows the total amount of debt in the U.S. through the last 100 years. Now imagine where we'll be 10 years from now, or 50 years from now.

WHO DO WE OWE ALL THIS MONEY TO?

Some people think that because we're the United States, we can simply declare that we don't want to pay back the money we borrowed, close the books, and point missiles at anyone who says otherwise. Unfortunately, the value of our currency depends on our ability to pay the interest on the national debt. Should we stop doing so, dollars you hold so dear would become worthless, quite literally, overnight. (We talked about his in Chapter 1. It might be worth re-reading that section if this is still confusing).

The loans to the US government are made in the form of Treasury Bonds. Because the US has never defaulted on a loan (we have a perfect credit rating), US Treasury Bonds are considered among the safest investments in the world. For this reason, they typically have a lower return than many other investments, but the world views this as a low-risk investment, so the returns are also equally low. Anyone can buy Treasury

Bonds (contact your local stock broker, they'll show you how. Many banks will also sell them, or you can buy them directly from the government). Foreign banks, governments, private corporations, and the citizens of the world are responsible for lending the $9 trillion dollars we currently owe today through these bonds.

The U.S. debt in the hands of foreign governments is about 25% of the total. Some argue that this exposes the United States to potential financial and political risks, including the idea that foreign governments may simply decide to stop purchase more bonds (effectively, not lending us any more money), or selling their existing bonds on the market for less than people can buy them from the U.S. (again, effectively making it difficult for the U.S. to borrow more money).

Another interesting note about our debt obligation is that 20% of the total national debt has an agreement attached that it will be repaid in foreign currency (not dollars). As we learned in the chapter about inflation, this puts the U.S. at a serious economic disadvantage, since a rapidly-declining dollar means our debt becomes more and more burdensome. It also means the United States can't simply "print more money" to clear the obligation.

ISN'T DEBT JUST THE NATURE OF GOVERNMENT?

Yes and no. It's not uncommon for a country to take on debt to cover costs (just like it's not uncommon for corporations to use debt as a tool). What we need to examine is whether or not the government can keep up with the trend, and how it compares to the rest of the world.

Of the roughly 162 countries in the world, 64 of them have a positive account balance (no debt whatsoever). China actually leads the world with nearly $2 trillion in cash surplus. Japan, Germany, Russia, and Saudi Arabia each have more than a trillion dollars in the bank. The US is dead-last in terms of overall debt, with a $9 trillion total (which we talked about above). Just behind us is Spain (with $980 billion) and the UK (with $570 billion). In other words, we carry nearly 10 times more debt than even the second-worst offender on the debt list. In fact, most of the countries who carry a negative balance are from Africa, south America, or the poorer remnants of the former soviet union. We're not in good company.

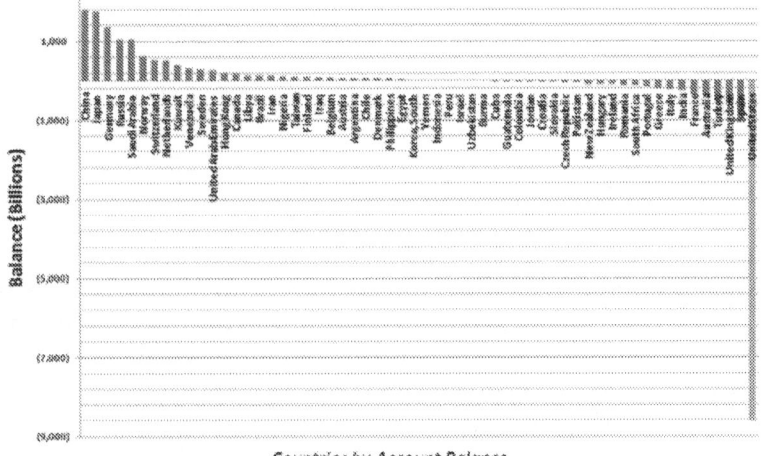

Countries by Account Balance

CHAPTER 6: THE STOCK MARKET

—

PRIVATE COMPANIES VS. PUBLIC COMPANIES

Private companies are what we usually think of when we talk about "a business". If you were to start your own company, it would be "private". Your only obligations as a business owner are to make sure you are treating your employees fairly according to the laws and to pay your taxes to the IRS. You do need to keep accounting records, but only so you can prove to the IRS that you paid them the correct amount. The "value" of your company is whatever you can convince someone to buy it for. In fact, you can sell the company to whomever you wish, whenever you wish, and for whatever amount of money you're willing to accept. You don't even have to sell the entire company, you can issue "shares" in your company and sell them. However, if you want to sell all or part of your company, you have to find the buyer yourself, and in order to agree on a price, the buyer will probably want to do a lot of research on your company (sales history, accounting practices, the market you're in, how much money you pay your employees, etc.). Of course, you don't have to show anyone this information (it's your company), but without it, you'll have a difficult time attracting an interested buyer.

When shopping for a way to sell a company, often times a larger organization will decide they want to "go public" instead. They're still selling the company, but they'll be selling it through a marketplace that's already been set up for buying and selling companies. This marketplace is called a "stock exchange". In order for a company to be listed on the "stock exchange" they go through what's known as an Initial Public Offering (IPO). Think of this as the process they go through to sell their private company to the public (or, in other words, to convert a private company to a public company).

During the IPO, the stock exchange rules will mandate that all of the information about the company be organized in a specific way. They will demand all historical accounting information, sales records, profits, losses, operating expenses, etc. The company will agree to publish this information every quarter and make it available for everyone to see. Because it's such a tightly controlled standard, it's a very expensive process for a company to go public and continue to maintain the level of records required. However, if you, Joe public, were going to invest in a company, you'd want to see all of that information first, right?

To summarize, the difference between a public company and a private company is that the public company participates in a marketplace wherein anyone can buy and sell shares of that company. A private company must find their own buyers and sellers, and is not required to adhere to any particular reporting standard (except that required by the IRS for basic tax purposes).

STOCK EXCHANGES

The "stock exchange" provides a place for companies to report all of the operating information to the public. This gives the public (you and I) a "one stop shop" for finding good companies to invest in. The stock exchange dictates what information the company needs to report, when it must be reported, and other technicalities the company must abide by.

The stock exchange is also responsible for matching buyers with sellers. If, after reading all of the financial information about a company, you decide you'd like to invest ("buy" part of that company) you can send your money to the "stock exchange" and they'll issue you a "stock certificate" in the company you're interested in. Think of the stock exchange as the "Wal-mart" of companies. You go to Wal-mart to buy products from thousands of different companies – you go to the stock exchange to buy shares in thousands of different companies.

There are several stock exchanges a company can choose to use when they decide they want to go public. The New York Stock Exchange (NYSE) and the NASDAQ are probably two you've probably heard of. The NASDAQ tends to cater more towards technology companies. Each exchange has different standards and requirements.

FOR EVERY BUYER THERE'S A SELLER

When we talk about the stock exchange being the marketplace for buying and selling public companies, we need to understand how this process works.

Orders enter the stock market through a stock broker (or a "brokerage firm") who is a member of the stock exchange. From there, the order flows down to the "floor brokers". They pick up the order and take it to the specific spot on the "floor" where that particular company is traded. This location is known as the "trading post", and there's a person here who matches the buyers with the sellers. Of course, this is all done through computers.

When you look at the "price" of a stock, it's always a single number. What you're actually looking at is the last price the stock traded for (it can change many times a second, so it's generally a good indicator of how much a share is worth).

The actual process of buying and selling stock is done through a live auction. That law of supply and demand from Chapter 1 really comes into play here. If you can imagine walking into a paperclip market and finding literally thousands of people selling paperclips and thousands of people wanting to buy paperclips. All of the paperclips are identical; the only goal is to match the buyers with the sellers. You look up to a giant board where it says the last paperclip sold for $0.10, and the one before that sold for $0.09, and the one before that sold for $0.08.

The price of paperclips is going up, but we, being smart paperclip investors, just don't believe for a minute a paperclip is worth $0.10. You write down your offer, $0.09, on a piece of paper and hold it over your head. The sellers are laughing at you. They see the last paperclip just sold for $0.10 and the price has been going up fast! They're all asking $0.11 and $0.12. Except now there's a problem. It's been a few minutes and nobody is buying at those prices. In fact, nobody is even offering $0.10 anymore. Maybe that last trade was a fluke. The sellers are getting nervous. Some need the money pretty quick (maybe they got a hot tip that the price of staples is about to go up, and they need to sell their paperclips quickly so they can buy staples instead). One of the sellers caves and lowers his price to match the highest bidder (that's you! $0.09!) and the deal is made. The price on "the board" changes to show that the last paperclip just sold for $0.09. Several other people were willing to sell them for $0.09 as well, and now the sellers are nervous that their paperclips aren't worth the $0.11 and $0.12 they were asking, so a few drop their price to $0.10. The buyers previously offering $0.09, worried that this might be just a temporary reduction in price, raise their offer to $0.10 and the sales are made. The board changes again. Paperclips are back to $0.10.

This is a simple example, but it's exactly how the whole process works, except in the real stock market it's all done through computers. Your stock broker is responsible for placing your buy and sell orders for you, while also managing the price you're willing to pay or sell for. Several stock brokers today have no human interaction between you and the actual stock market (sometimes they're referred to as "electronic stock brokers"). You can manage all of your trades in real time directly through their web-site. Your orders are passed automatically into the market and fulfilled based on your parameters. You can track the status of your orders through the whole process.

Humans play only a limited role in the stock trading process in most exchanges, but the process and the auction are still played out the same way.

THE DOW AND OTHER INDEXES

Investors like to see the "big picture" when they're trying to make decisions about what to do with their money, thus the "index" was born. The idea behind an index is to present an average on how a bunch of different stocks are doing.

The Dow Jones Industrial Average (DJIA, or "The Dow") is probably the best known index. In fact, much of our perceived economic health is based on this index. The Dow was created in the 1800's as a way to gauge the overall performance of the American industrial companies. The Dow is made up of the average stock price of 30 of the largest public companies in the U.S. Only a few have anything to do with heavy industry anymore, however. Examples of companies that participate in the Dow 30 include AT&T, GM, IBM, McDonalds, Microsoft, Boeing, Wal-Mart, and Pfizer.

There's actually a complicated formula used to compute the average. Don't worry about that for now, just know that the result of the formula gives us the final number you see on the news every night. Critics of the Dow argue that it's not a true reflection of the American economic picture because the 30 companies that are used to compute the index can and are swapped out with stronger companies if they start performing poorly. Thus, they argue, the Dow is nothing more than a marketing gimmick to show constant strength in the American economy over the long-term.

Of course, the Dow isn't the only index we have. There are hundreds of others. Examples include the Nasdaq-100 (top 100 technology companies), the S&P 500 (average of 500 major companies selected by Standards & Poor's), the NYSE Composite Index (all of the companies traded by the New York Stock Exchange), etc. There are also thousands of smaller indexes for tracking specific economic activity (for example, the AG index is designed to track the performance of the agriculture industry).

MUTUAL FUNDS AND ETF'S

The biggest challenge for the small investor is finding companies that meet their requirements. There are so many things to consider when choosing stocks to invest in (risk, size of the company, management potential, the industry they're in, their profit potential, etc.) that it's nearly impossible to build an investment strategy yourself without investing hundreds of hours in research. The "mutual fund" is designed to solve this problem.

A mutual fund is a professionally-managed collection of investments. The "fund manager" will decide on a strategy for their fund (example: they might choose to only invest in medium-risk companies involved in mining natural resources). They would pool the money from lots of different investors to buy stocks, bonds, real estate, or other investments related to the strategy they've chosen, and the investors are given shares in the mutual fund rather than the individual investments. Of course, as the value of the investments go up, so does the value of the mutual fund shares (and vice-versa if the investments do poorly). Because you can off-load the research to professionals and simply identity the types of risk you're willing to take or the industries you want to invest in, mutual funds are a great way for individual investors to play the stock market.

An Exchange Traded Fund (or ETF) allows you to buy things on the stock market ("paper investments") that would be otherwise impossible. For example, there's a "Gold ETF" (Symbol: GLD) that allows you buy and sell gold as though it were stock in a company. Of course, gold isn't a company, it's a thing. But as the value of gold goes up, the value of a share of the gold ETF goes up as well. You can effectively buy and sell gold without ever seeing or touching it. ETFs aren't limited just to trading physical assets, though. There are ETFs designed to make money in particular market conditions. For example, there's an ETF designed to increase in value as the Dow goes down, and decrease in value as the Dow goes up (amusingly, the symbol for that ETF is "DOG"). ETFs allow investors to get very creative in finding ways to make money in changing market conditions, they also allow small-time investors the ability to invest in resources they may not be able to manage otherwise.

MAKING MONEY WHEN THE MARKET GOES DOWN

I thought it worth talking a little about how it's possible to make money when the market goes down because I wanted to point out that a marketing that's going up doesn't necessarily mean everyone is losing money. In fact, there's an old rule in economics that says "for every winner there's a loser and for every loser a winner". If this rule is true, then someone must be making money when the market crashes.

Certainly formulating a strategy for a down-market profit would be beyond the scope of this book, but it's worth mentioning a few of the things investors use to make money when a stock, or the entire market, heads south. First, there's ETFs (mentioned above) which can be designed to make money in "inverse market conditions". Options are another way (we'll talk about that in a second), and "shorting" a stock is the one most people think of.

When you "short" a stock, you're making a big bet that the value of that stock will decline (if it does, you'll make money). The process works like this: Rather than buying shares in a company, we'll borrow them from someone who already owns them and sell them (the money for the sale is deposited into our account. Let's say it was $10,000). We do have to give the shares back eventually, but we can choose when to do that. If the price of the stock goes down by, say, 20%, we'll buy the shares on the open market (at 20% less than we sold them for -- $8,000) and give the shares back to the person who borrowed them from. This leaves us with a net profit of $2,000. Of course, if the price of the stock goes up instead of down, we'll be forced to buy them (so we can return them to the lender) for more money than we sold them for. We will have lost money. At some point, if the price of a stock keeps going higher and higher, your broker will force you to buy the shares back and return them to the lender. The risk for them is that you won't be able to come up with the money and they'll be left holding the bag. In fact, most brokers won't let you "sell short" unless you've got other investments or cash to use as collateral in case the stock price goes up instead of down (your potential loss is unlimited).

OPTIONS

Up until now, we've talked about trading actual securities (stocks, bonds, real estate, etc.) – something with real value. Options are not a security. They have no physical thing behind them. Instead, options are a contract (or a "right") to engage in some specific transaction at a future date.

A simple example of an "options contract" might be Jim, who believes at some point in the near future, jelly beans are going to double. Let's assume that today a jelly bean is worth about $0.05. However, Jim has his money wrapped up in other investments, so he can't afford to just run out and buy a bunch of jelly beans and wait for them to go up in value. Besides, he doesn't have anywhere to keep them. On the other hand, we've got Sally, who happens to have lots of Jelly beans, but doesn't believe they're going to go up in value like Jim does. Jim approaches her with a deal.

Jim wants the *option* to buy 100,000 of Sally's jelly beans for $0.06 each any time (his choice) within the next 6 months. In exchange for this "option" Jim will pay Sally $500 in cash, right now, and she can keep the money regardless of what Jim chooses to do. Jim and Sally agree on the deal, and they now have a legal contract.

If the value of jelly beans double like Jim thinks it will, rather than sell her jelly beans on the open market for $0.10 each, Jim will "exercise" his option and Sally will be forced to sell 100,000 of her jelly beans to Jim for the previously agreed $0.06 – Jim will, of course, turn around and sell them for $0.10 each. He might not even take possession of the jelly beans (he would probably send the buyer to pick them up directly from Sally, that way he didn't have to be bothered with storing them). For the cost of the $500 option, Jim has created a huge profit.

($7,000 to buy them and $10,000 to sell them = $3,000 in cash for his $500 investment. That's a 600% profit!) If Jim had simply purchased the jelly beans from the beginning for the market price of $0.05 and sold them 6 months later for $0.10, he would have only made 100% profit, and his cash would have been tied up in jelly beans the whole time.

On the other hand, if the value of jelly beans never goes higher than $0.06, Jim will have no reason to exercise his option, since he could buy the jelly beans from anyone for the same price, or less. Sally still keeps the $500 and ends up on the winning end of the transaction. Jim loses 100% of his (relatively small) investment.

An "option" in the stock-market world works the same way. The exchanges have created a marketplace for investors to buy and sell options contracts tied to stocks, bonds, ETFs, and other investments. They don't ever have to take control of the investments, but they do have the *option* to buy or sell them at pre-agreed prices within a pre-agreed time frame. Options allow investors to *control* large portions of stock (just like Jim controlled a lot of jelly beans) without actually having to buy them first).

More detail in how these contracts work is well beyond the scope of this book, but that should give you some idea of what an option actually is.

CHAPTER 7: THE DEBT-FUELED ECONOMY

WHY DEBT MAKES THE ECONOMY TICK

The world economy has been growing a rate that far exceeds the population and income growth rates. The reason is simple: We've figured out new ways to leverage debt so we can buy more. From a personal standpoint, I think we all understand that the more you put on the credit card, the more "stuff" you can buy. The more stuff you buy, the better the overall economy does. Buying more stuff means more stuff has to be made, which means more jobs – it also means more debt for you! Simple, right?

DERIVATIVES: HOW BANKS LEVERAGE DEBT

On a much larger scale, banks play the same game with what are known as "derivatives". Derivatives are the ability to borrow money based on the assets you have as collateral. While the term is usually only in reference to banks, average citizens can play in the derivative game, too. Most of us don't have a stomach for that kind of risk, but just to help you understand what they are and how they work, here's a real example of how a person (like you and I) could get themselves in trouble with derivatives.

Let's say you open a stock-market trading account with Morgan Stanley. You send them $50,000 and they deposit that money into your account. You use that money to buy $50,000 in stocks (Microsoft, GM, McDonalds... all your favorites). You now have assets worth $50k. The bank (Morgan Stanley) will lend you up to 50% of the value of those assets (if you don't pay them back, they'll sell your stock to cover it. If the value of your stock goes down, there's enough "room" in there -- 50% -- that they can always sell off your assets if things start going badly in the stock market). This is called a "margin loan"... You decide to do this, so Morgan Stanley writes you a check for $25,000.

You decide to take your $25,000 and open another investment account at Ameritrade. You deposit your money, buy more stocks, and, once again, take out another margin loan. They send you a check for $12,500. You take this check to E-Trade and open another brokerage account, buy more stock, and take out ANOTHER margin loan for $6,250....

You see where we're going. The term for this is "leveraging up". Your $50,000 allowed you to own nearly $100,000 REAL assets. If you think this feels like a pyramid scheme, you're right. The dark side is that if the "bottom falls out" and your $50,000 suddenly becomes worth $10,000 (maybe McDonalds goes out of business?) the entire house of cards will collapse on top of you. Every loan will declare the entire balance "due" because you no longer have the underlying asset to back it all up. We have, in effect, tricked the banks into lending us money by making them think they have the right to an asset if we default, when in reality, we've already promised that asset to someone else. It's "risky business", but it works well in a booming economy.

Remember, this is not the stuff of financial gurus. This is something you could do today with horrible credit. There are no checks and balances tracking where the money goes or why – you control all of that, and you don't need good credit because there's always the illusion of an asset backing your next "level" of investment. In reality, there's only one asset (the one on the bottom), but the other banks don't know that. All they see is cold, hard cash.

Banks, on the other hand, have very good credit. They get much better lending terms than you are I. While you and I can leverage (on average) 50% of the value of our assets, banks can often leverage 125% (or more) of their underlying asset.

Mortgages usually sit "at the bottom" of this house of cards that banks like to build. They're the foundation of the debt-scheme because they're safe, secure, and they represent real property and real returns. They're solid. In fact, mortgages are so well respected in the financial industry, a bank could easily leverage more than $3 million in "derivative investments" with a $400,000 mortgage sitting at the bottom. Sometimes they'll even buy a mortgage with the money derived from another mortgage (making it even harder to find the underlying asset the whole thing is based on).

Occasionally, mortgages (or other investments) do go bad. Banks have enough money they can shift things around until it all balanced out again. They're pretty good at playing the game (they've been doing it for a long time) – the banks simply hope (and bet) that an unusual number of home loans won't default at the same time.

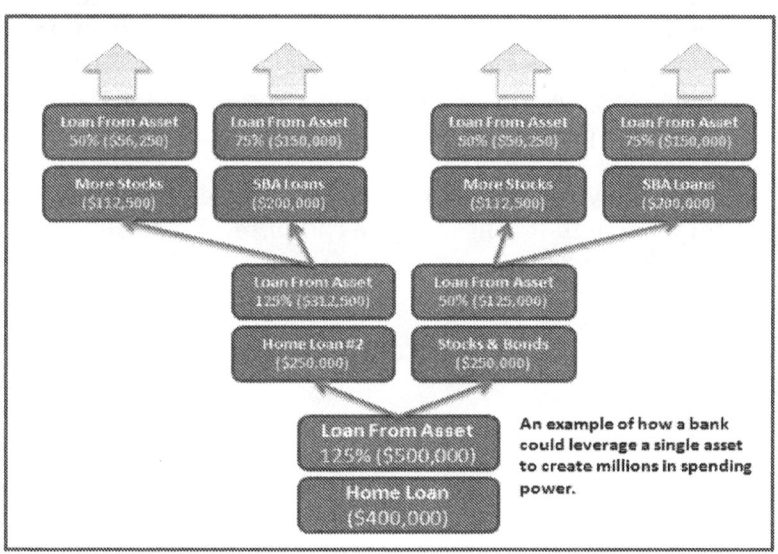

An example of how a bank could leverage a single asset to create millions in spending power.

WHY DOES DEBT MATTER IN A GLOBAL ECONOMY?

Just to put this in perspective, the size (or value) of the stock market is about $51 trillion. The size of the derivative market is about $480 trillion. This means banks have figured out a way to leverage nearly 1,000% in assets that they don't have the money to pay for (the same way we tricked our banks into lending us money for collateral that had already been promised to someone else). It also means that for every $400,000 home loan, there's as much as $4 million in "derived" investments floating through the economy.

As long as the economy continues to do well, there's actually no problem with this. The "bubble" created will continue to get bigger as they come up with more and more creative ways to borrow money against this "shadowy assets". The more they borrow (and spend), the better the economy does. The better the economy does, the more they *can* borrow.

Remember, though, it only takes the prick of a pin to bring it all down. If an unusual number of assets "default" (or suddenly become worthless), or if the economy slows too quickly, the whole charade will be over in a matter of months. The aftermath will not be pretty.

This is the very essence of the "debt fueled economy". It's a story worth telling around the campfire. You're bound to scare someone.

FINAL COMMENTS

———

Hopefully by the time you reach this chapter you're feeling confident in being able to understand and make sense of the headlines we see every night on the news. I believe if you look at everything from the perspective of "supply and demand" (as discussed in the first chapter), the economy as a whole will make a lot more sense.

I would encourage you to always ask yourself the question of "why" when someone in power makes a decision. Why are they doing this? Who will benefit? Are there other possible motivations they may not be talking about? If you don't understand something, often times asking yourself these questions will lead you to an answer.

Always remember there are millions of people out there who claim to understand the principals discussed in this book, but fail to really grasp how they affect their everyday life. I fear that politicians, lawyers, judges, and others who help to shape our society and our laws are severely lacking in their understanding of these basics. Hopefully, after having read this book, you're in a position to help teach others. I would strongly encourage you to do so. The consequences of an American people who do not understand these things are immense.

www.ingramcontent.com/pod-product-compliance
Lightning Source LLC
Chambersburg PA
CBHW021922170526
45157CB00005B/2144